THE BALVIHAR BOOK OF PICTURE PARABLES

Script and Illustrations
Bharati Sukhatankar

CENTRAL CHINMAYA MISSION TRUST

First Edition December 2001 - 3,000 copies
Reprint from April 2003 to December 2014 - aprx 14,000 copies
Reprint October 2017 - 2000 copies

Published by:
Chinmaya Prakashan
The Publications Division of
Central Chinmaya Mission Trust
Sandeepany Sadhanalaya
Saki Vihar Road, Mumbai 400072, India
Tel.: +91-22-2857 2367, 2857 5806 Fax: +91-22-2857 3065
Email: ccmtpublications@chinmayamission.com
Website: www.chinmayamission.com

Distribution Centre in USA:
Chinmaya Mission West
Publications Division
560 Bridgetown Pike, Langhorne, PA 19053, USA
Tel.: 1-888-CMW-READ, (215) 396-0390 Fax: (215) 396-9710
Email: publications@chinmayamission.org
Website: www.chinmayapublications.org

Printed by: Usha Multigraphs Pvt. Ltd., Mumbai, India
ISBN: 978-81-7597-023-6

Foreword

The Bal Vihar magazine has played a vital role in the history of the Chinmaya Mission. Started in 1969 by Pujya Gurudev swami Chinmayananda it was aimed at moulding the minds of the children and thereby laying the foundation for producing men and women of strong moral character, upholding the timeless values of Indian culture. Pujya Gurudev's idea was to "catch them young".

Towards this goal, Bal Vihar has worked for over thirty years. Much valuable material has been published so far and so it was decided that in this, the 50th year of the Chinmaya Movement, it would be a good idea to reprint a series of all colour Bal Vihar books under different titles. this would strengthen the grass root level activities and help the Bal Vihar children and sevaks

I commend the work done by the Bal Vihar team and wish them all success in their ongoing efforts.

Mumbai

December 2001   (Swami Tejomayananda)

EDITOR'S NOTE

These Picture Parables are not original stories. They have been taken from traditional sources and from folk tales the world over. The stories are straight and simple and our attempt has been to "tell" not "teach", as Gurudev used to say.

Many of the parables have been sent to us by one of Gurudev's oldest devotees, Urmila, from Germany. All the stories have been adapted to the Indian milieu and have appeared in the Bal Vihar issues from 1999-2001.

Bal Vihar offers this as a tribute to Priya Gurudev, Swami Chinmayananda, in the 50th year of the Chinmaya Movement.

Mumbai

December 2001

Swamini Aaradhanananda
(formerly Brni. Vividisa Chaitanya)

INDEX

10

A rabbit who heard this was disgusted.
But what a beautifully bushy tail you have_
_ Mine is short and stumpy. SIGH!
A mole heard the rabbit sighing.
What are you complaining about? Look at me. I am blind.
The horse, having heard all, said_
HE WHO CONSIDERS HIMSELF THE MOST UNLUCKY IS SURELY THE MOST FOOLISH!

Right. I'll get the calves first. Then you eat the brahmin.

Their argument woke up the sleeping brahmin.

Nonsense. I am very hungry. I will eat the brahmin first. Then you take the calves.

A rakshasa! A thief!

Om Sri Ram Jai Ram Jai Jai Ram...

As for the thief—

Be off, you rascal, before I beat you black and blue!

The rakshasa fled immediately.

WHEN YOUR ENEMIES QUARREL AMONG THEMSELVES, YOU STAND TO GAIN!

So he set about preparing a trap for Bhondu.

What a kind and wonderful man. He has specially put peanuts for me in this pot.

And into the pot went Bhondu's hand.

Full of peanuts, Bhondu's hand got stuck in the pot.

But Bhondu didn't. And he was caught by the animal catcher. All for a handful of peanuts.

All that Bhondu had to do is let go of the peanuts and pull his hand out.

Bleeding and tired and utterly exhausted, they refused to carry him. So he had to sit down.
All the while, those Red Indians kept coming on. He pleaded with his feet to resume their work, but they just would not budge. They mocked him —

You have never really cared much about us. But now you realise our worth.

What does it matter to us if the head is scalped? Tell your clever head to run. We are very tired.

Okay then. But with the head gone, you feet won't be of any use either.

When the feet realised the truth of this, they started running faster than ever — till the man finally escaped the Red Indians.

Phew! Made it!

If the head is dead, what use are the feet? We are one dependent on the other.

Sukrut was touched by the plight of the man.

True, we haven't eaten vegetables for several days. But this man hasn't eaten at all.

Here are some coins, brother. Buy yourself some food and eat it.

So you're back, Sukrut. Come, let's see what you have brought and what we'll eat today.

Sukrut prepared himself for the wrath of the master.

We will eat a thin lentil soup and rice. I am sorry, Gurudev. I met a man on the road who had not eaten for many days and I gave the coins to him.

Well done! Shabash! You have learnt your lessons well. What better action could you have performed? By feeding the beggar, you have fed God.

MONEY IS BEST USED WHEN IT IS USED TO SERVE THOSE WHO NEED IT.

But the other jackals of the forest were not impressed. They got together in a far off corner.

What do you make of our new king?

There's something fishy there.

I have an idea

According to plan, that evening, all the jackals started howling together.

The other animals pounced upon the jackal and killed him.

HOOOWLLLLL

You cheat!

The false king could not resist joining in the chorus and gave himself away.

TRYING TO FOOL OTHERS CAN LAND YOU INTO TROUBLE!

Our fate is so similar. We are both plunged into fire and then we are hammered up. The blows are so painful. SIGH. But I don't make as loud a noise as you do.
Not so bad for you, my friend--
--for you are beaten by a hammer which is not your kin.
Think of me- I have to suffer blows from a hammer made of iron-- blows from my own brother-
- my own flesh and blood. Believe me, it is much more painful.
THE PAIN THAT OTHERS GIVE TO US, WE CAN TOLERATE. BUT THE PAIN GIVEN TO US BY OUR OWN BELOVED ONES, O THAT IS REALLY TERRIBLE!

The goat hesitated.

I am not sure if I can spare it...

O come on. What are you afraid of? Besides, that fox there will be my surety.

In that case I will never give you the wheat. For you are fleet footed and will run away—

—and the fox will simply eat me up!

It is foolishness to lend when you know you won't get back what is owed.

To his great surprise, he heard a voice saying —

Before you offer me any sweets, learn to help yourself. Unload the cart and make it light.

Put some stones in the slush. Use a strong stick as a lever and then get the mule to heave.

The cartman acted on the instructions of the voice. Soon the cart was on the road, rolling along.

Where did the voice come from? Was it from within me?

It's true. There's nothing like helping yourself.

As time went by, the chick grew into a beautiful peacock.
He danced with delight...
... and roamed the farmyard at will. And he observed—
These chickens are always pecking.
kit kit
kit
They can't help it. That's the way they are. Why should I be unhappy because of someone else's bad nature?
kit
kit
kit kit
With that he learnt to keep himself happy and contented.
DON'T ALLOW OTHERS TO DICTATE YOUR HAPPINESS!

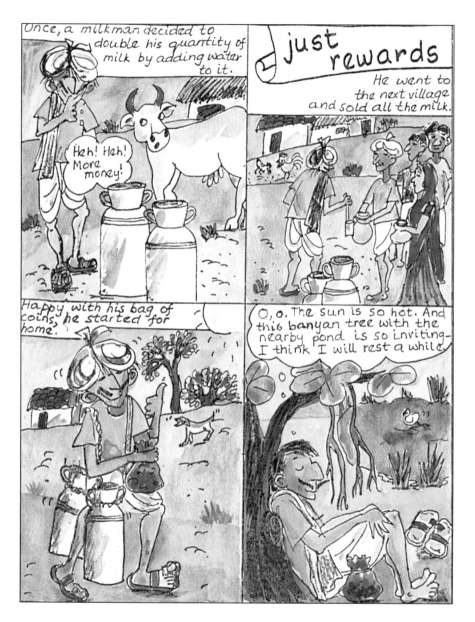

Balvihar, an international kids' monthly of the Chinmaya Mission, has carved a niche for itself by winning The Best NGO mag Award twice in a row! "We shall through this magazine, build bridges of love and understanding everywhere, and leave this world a better place than what our parents have given us!" So stated Pujya Gurudev, Swami Chinmayananda in the introductory issue. The magazine, replete with kid-friendly nuggets on Indian traditions, festivals and spiritual practices lovingly imparts 'sanskars' to the kids, without being preachy. The magazine, balances legends and stories on Indian heritage with puzzles, jokes, brain-teasers and activity pages. There are also exclusive pages for the kids, by the kids, showcasing their innocent and honest expressions.

Pujya Guruji Swami Tejomayananda urges, "Give your kids values instead of valuables!" His motto for the magazine, 'Love, Learning, Laughter,' reflects in its pages.

To subscribe please visit www.chinmayakids.org

There is no doubt that in today's world the most powerful and effective means of communication across all borders is the Internet. Thus the Chinmaya Mission has created a delightful, child-friendly website, rich in content and graphics, to impart to young hearts and minds the wisdom of the ancient Scriptures, which till today provide a strong foundation of ideals, virtues and values that speak to character. This effort is in line with the Chinmaya Mission's mission statement: "To provide to individuals of any background the wisdom of Vedanta along with practical means for spiritual growth and happiness, enabling them to become positive contributors to society". You and your child are cordially invited to visit and enjoy this website. www.chinmayakids.org.